P9-CQE-144

SandCastle™

Antonyms

Did I Hear a Hello from Above or Below?

Mary Elizabeth Salzmann

Consulting Editor, Diane Craig, M.A./Reading Specialist

ABDO Publishing Company

10/08

Published by ABDO Publishing Company, 4940 Viking Drive, Edina, Minnesota 55435.

Printed in the United States.

Credits
Edited by: Pam Price
Curriculum Coordinator: Nancy Tuminelly
Cover and Interior Design and Production: Mighty Media
Photo Credits: BananaStock Ltd., Big Cheese Photo, Brand X Pictures, Comstock, JupiterImages Corporation, Purestock, ShutterStock, Wewerka Photography

Library of Congress Cataloging-in-Publication Data
Salzmann, Mary Elizabeth, 1968-
  Did I hear a hello from above or below? / Mary Elizabeth Salzmann.
    p. cm. -- (Antonyms)
  ISBN-13: 978-1-59928-716-4
  ISBN-10: 1-59928-716-1
  1. English language--Synonyms and antonyms--Juvenile literature. I. Title.

PE1591.S26 2007
428.1--dc22
                              2006032018

SandCastle™ books are created by a professional team of educators, reading specialists, and content developers around five essential components—phonemic awareness, phonics, vocabulary, text comprehension, and fluency—to assist young readers as they develop reading skills and strategies and increase their general knowledge. All books are written, reviewed, and leveled for guided reading, early reading intervention, and Accelerated Reader® programs for use in shared, guided, and independent reading and writing activities to support a balanced approach to literacy instruction.

Let Us Know

SandCastle would like to hear your stories about reading this book. What is your favorite page? Was there something hard that you needed help with? Share the ups and downs of learning to read. We want to hear from you! To get posted on the ABDO Publishing Company Web site, send us e-mail at:

sandcastle@abdopublishing.com

SandCastle Level: Transitional

Antonyms are words that have opposite meanings.

Here is a good way to remember what an antonym is:

antonym

=

opposite

Also, **antonym** and **opposite** both start with vowels.

3

antonyms

Ava and Gabrielle use snorkeling
gear to look below the sea.

antonyms

At the playground, Justin swings high above the ground.

antonyms

In class, Noah sits in the front row.

On car trips, Mackenzie sits in the back seat.

Jen and Steven have fun when their grandparents come for a visit.

antonyms

Eric and Caroline go to the museum to look at dinosaur bones.

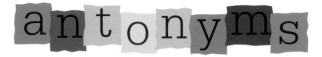

Adam and Wyatt jump off the side of the pool.

antonyms

Sierra is first in line to get on the school bus.

antonyms

Becca and Timothy slide down the hill. Then they will drag the sled back up the hill and slide down again!

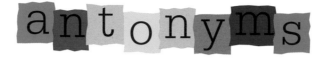

antonyms

Evelyn is at the mall shopping for new clothes. Her old clothes are getting too small for her.

Katelyn is on a narrow
bridge that crosses a
wide river.

antonyms

Gavin and his mom wait near the train. It will take them to visit his grandma who lives far away.

Antonym Activity

down up

come go

back front

new old

Antonym Pairs

above — below

back — front

come — go

down — up

far — near

narrow — wide

new — old

off — on

In each box on page 20, choose the antonym that describes the picture.

21

Words I Know

Nouns
A noun is a person, place, or thing.

bones, 9
bridge, 17
car, 7
class, 6
clothes, 15
dinosaur, 9
fun, 8
gear, 4
grandma, 19
grandparents, 8

ground, 5
hill, 13
line, 11
mall, 15
mom, 19
museum, 9
playground, 5
pool, 10
river, 17
row, 6

school bus, 11
sea, 4
seat, 7
side, 10
sled, 13
snorkeling, 4
train, 19
trips, 7
visit, 8

Adjectives
An adjective describes something.

away, 19
back, 7
first, 11
front, 6

her, 15
his, 19
narrow, 17
new, 15

old, 15
small, 15
their, 8
wide, 17

Words I Know

Verbs
A verb is an action or being word.

are, 15

come, 8

crosses, 17

drag, 13

get(ting), 11, 15

go, 9

have, 8

is, 11, 15, 17

jump, 10

lives, 19

look, 4, 9

shopping, 15

sits, 6, 7

slide, 13

swings, 5

take, 19

use, 4

visit, 19

wait, 19

will, 13, 19

Proper Nouns
A proper noun is the name of a person, place, or thing.

Adam, 10

Ava, 4

Becca, 13

Caroline, 9

Eric, 9

Evelyn, 15

Gabrielle, 4

Gavin, 19

Jen, 8

Justin, 5

Katelyn, 17

Mackenzie, 7

Noah, 6

Sierra, 11

Steven, 8

Timothy, 13

Wyatt, 10

About SandCastle™

A professional team of educators, reading specialists, and content developers created the SandCastle™ series to support young readers as they develop reading skills and strategies and increase their general knowledge. The SandCastle™ series has four levels that correspond to early literacy development in young children. The levels are provided to help teachers and parents select appropriate books for young readers.

Emerging Readers
(no flags)

Beginning Readers
(1 flag)

Transitional Readers
(2 flags)

Fluent Readers
(3 flags)

These levels are meant only as a guide. All levels are subject to change.

To see a complete list of SandCastle™ books and other nonfiction titles from ABDO Publishing Company, visit www.abdopublishing.com or contact us at: 4940 Viking Drive, Edina, Minnesota 55435 • 1-800-800-1312 • fax: 1-952-831-1632